D1168966

STUDENT SURVIVAL GUIDE

How to Work Smarter, Not Harder

College Entrance Examination Board
New York

Copies of this book may be ordered from your local bookseller or from College Board Publications, Box 886, New York, New York 10101-0886. The price is $4.95.

Editorial inquiries concerning this book should be directed to Editorial Office, The College Board, 45 Columbus Avenue, New York, New York 10023-6992.

Library of Congress Catalog Number: 91-071866

ISBN: 0-87447-401-9

Printed in the United States of America

9 8 7 6 5 4 3 2 1

CONTENTS

WORK SMARTER, NOT HARDER

Getting Off To the Right Start

What's the first big challenge you have to overcome if you want to study more efficiently, learn more productively, and have more time for fun? If you are one of the vast majority--the "I'll-do-it-later,just-let-me-sleep-five-minutes-more,no-time-for-breakfast" procrastinator--your day probably begins with a frantic dash that gets you to your first class breathless and disorganized.

If you've ever ridden a horse or run a race, you know how important it is to get off to a smooth start. The same holds true for success in school. Getting off to the right start is half the battle--on time, unhassled, with the necessary books and completed assignments for that day's courses.

Your Timetable

How long does it take you to get going in the morning? Twenty minutes, forty-five minutes, an hour? Write down your estimate:

_____ minutes

Some people get going faster than others, but whether you are a speed demon or a dawdler, the chances are that you have underestimated the amount of time you need to get up, wash, brush your teeth, put on your clothes, make the bed, eat breakfast, and get to class on time. But it's easy enough to find out just how much time it actually takes and to set up a schedule to suit you.

Time-Study Experiment

Run a time-study experiment the first chance you have. Make a date with yourself for the next free Saturday, Sunday, or holiday--and go through *every* step of your normal daily morning routine from the moment the alarm wakes you to your arrival at your first class. Here's how to conduct your experiment:

- Do whatever you usually do at a comfortable pace

- Time each and *every* activity

- Record the amount of time each activity takes on the following chart

Activity	Number of Minutes
Lingering in bed after the alarm goes off	_____
Bathroom chores (brushing teeth, etc.)	_____
Making the bed	_____
Getting dressed	_____
Grooming (combing hair, etc.)	_____
Daydreaming	_____
Listening to radio/TV	_____
Eating breakfast	_____
Gathering together note books, money, keys, etc.	_____
Getting from home/dorm to classroom	_____
_____	_____
_____	_____
_____	_____
_____	_____
_____	_____

Use the blank spaces to add any activities that are part of your routine but haven't been included in the list above.

You may have been surprised to discover how much time you need in the morning to get yourself going. Now that you know, you can set yourself a schedule that fits your rhythms and priorities. If you just can't jump out of bed the moment the alarm rings, then give yourself an extra ten minutes to loll in bed--but do it by setting the alarm to go off ten minutes earlier so you won't find yourself behind schedule before the day has even begun.

Time-Saving, Tension-Defusing Techniques

Here are some tips for saving precious minutes in the morning:

- Take your shower or bath before going to bed rather than waiting until morning.

- Decide what you're going to wear the night before and know where the clothes are so you won't have to hunt through your closet, drawers, or the basket full of unsorted clean laundry to find what you need.

- Before you go to bed, gather together the books and other things you'll need for school the next day and put them where you can pick them up handily on your way out in the morning.

Everyone has individual stumbling blocks that get in the way of starting the day off comfortably, so identify what yours are and decide how to avoid them, applying the same kinds of techniques outlined above.

Personal Checklist

Stumbling Block   **Time-Saver**

_____   _____

_____   _____

_____   _____

_____   _____

_____   _____

Don't let the humdrum details of life run you and spoil your fun. Make a time schedule that works for you. Getting to class, or wherever you have to be, on time relieves you of a lot of tension and gives you a headstart on getting the most out of the day. You'll look better because you're not frazzled, out of breath, unkempt. You will think better because you're not distracted by rushing and worrying about being late. The self-confidence that it gives you is bound to work to your advantage--in and out of school.

DATE, TIME, PLACE

Business executives and politicians are not the only people who need to keep day-to-day appointment calendars. You need one too to keep track of your own schedule--to know what you are going to be doing, when, and with whom.

Missing a meeting with your academic adviser, a band practice session, or even an appointment with the dentist are forms of self-sabotage. You anger the person who was expecting you, you end up angry with yourself--and you only have to reschedule those missed appointments for another time. So it makes sense to be where you are supposed to be at the right time on the right day. Just about everyone forgets an appointment now and then, but by carefully monitoring your calendar you can keep it to a minimum.

Write It Down

At this point you may wonder what in the world you have to write down in an appointment calendar. The answer is *lots*! Just think of the different things you do and people you see in the course of a week. Take a few minutes to write down the things that come to mind.

Separate the activities into several basic categories and you will probably find that you have quite a list under each. For example:

School

- due dates for term papers and exams
- drama club audition
- basketball/soccer/volleyball practice
- student government meeting
- band/chorus/orchestra practice
- study session with friend

Personal

- dinner with a friend
- tennis lesson
- driver's license renewal
- Friday night dance at the Y
- TV special you don't want to miss
- Saturday errands

Dates You Don't Want to Forget

- friends' and family's birthdays
- holiday parties
- school football team's home games
- rock concert later in the month
- parents' anniversary

Calendar Confidence

Knowing what you have to get done and setting a time for doing it eliminates confusion and wasted time. It separates chore time from *your* time. It lets you know just how much free time you have, which is the first step toward making the most of it.

The kind of appointment calendar you use will depend on your personality and preferences. Some people like a pocket-size date book with spaces for three or four days' appointments per page so that they can see what is on the schedule for a whole week when they turn to any double page. But that kind of calendar doesn't leave much room for writing in details. You may regularly have days that look like this:

Monday, March 1

> 10:00--meeting re work-study program
> 12:15--see Leslie in cafeteria to get
>   class notes
> 1:30--work on history midterm at
>   computer center
> 3:00--band practice
> 8:30--TV special on gymnastics/
>   must see!

If that's typical of your days, you may prefer a desk calendar with one page per day. The trouble with that kind of record is that you can't have it with you at all times. But just writing down what you have to do and when you have to do it helps fix it in your mind, so it's certainly better than not keeping a record at all.

One handy way to set up your appointment calendar is on a weekly or a monthly chart that can be attached with tape to the inside cover of your school notebook. Then you can always tell at a glance what is coming up in the days or weeks ahead.

See the following pages for weekly and monthly calendar formats that you might find convenient to use.

The weekly calendar gives you enough space for noting where you have to be and when you have to be there, plus room for miscellaneous notes to yourself.

You have less writing space on the monthly calendar but it has the advantage of letting you see at a glance what you have scheduled for several weeks at a time.

Weekly Calendar

Monday

    10:00--meeting re work-study program

    12:15--see Leslie in cafeteria to get class
        notes

    1:30--work on history midterm at
        computer center

    3:00--band practice

    8:30--TV special on gymnastics/must see!

Tuesday

Wednesday

Thursday

Friday

Saturday

Sunday

Notes

Monthly Calendar

Monday	Tuesday	Wednesday
10:00/wk-study meeting 12:15/Les.notes 1:30/history midterm 3:00/band 8:30/TV-gym		

Thursday	Friday	Saturday	Sunday

GET ORGANIZED FOR STUDYING

Whatever your immediate and long-range goals are for college and career, you can achieve them more easily and effectively by being well-organized. As a student, you want to get the most out of the time you spend doing school work--whether taking notes during a classroom lecture, doing research in the library, or studying in your own room.

Organizing your activities is a major step toward becoming more efficient and accomplishing all the things that are important to you--everything from homework, an after-school job or volunteer work to team practice, having fun with friends, or just spending some quiet time by yourself.

Getting Started

Your calendar is basically a schedule of your activities from day to day and week to week, so be sure to check it *every* day. Whether yours is a daily, weekly, or monthly schedule, don't toss it away when the time period is over. It's a record of your responsibilities and accomplishments, so file it to refer to when you're planning next semester's schedule or even preparing a job resume.

Organizing Study Space

Your first priority is to create a good space where you can concentrate. Don't kid yourself into thinking that you can concentrate on an assignment while sitting in the cafeteria surrounded by friends, or stretched out on the bed in your dorm while your roommate is having a pizza party. Your basic needs are:

- A quiet place with a minimum of visual distractions
- A comfortable place with good light
- A work surface large enough for your books, papers, and files

At the beginning of the semester, start a file folder for each course. Those folders will provide a handy permanent place to keep the papers and reference materials that you don't need for class every day but do want to refer to when you're studying or writing a report.

Managing Study Time

Put study time high on your priority list when planning your schedule. Make a realistic estimate of how many hours a week you'll need to keep up with all your assignments, block out study times in manageable segments, mark them on your schedule, and then treat them like the important appointments they are.

You need sufficient time to reach a logical cutoff point in any assignment. Allow enough time to accomplish a particular goal. Working in short ten- or fifteen-minute spurts gets in the way of efficiency. Plan to work a minimum of thirty to forty-five minutes at a time. And be sure to take a break at least every hour or hour and a half. If you try to work longer than that without interruption, your concentration and efficiency start to drop.

Pacing Yourself

At this point in your life you probably have a pretty accurate sense of your personal rhythm-- you know during what part of the day or evening you work most effectively and when your energy is at low ebb. Try to schedule study times when your ability to concentrate is at its peak. If you can, work *only* during those peak times.

If your program is too heavy to make that possible, save the easier, more routine assignments for your lower energy period. You may not have much control over the *amount* of school work to be done, but you're in the driver's seat when it comes to *pacing* that work, so give yourself the help you deserve.

Taking Study Notes

It is as helpful to take notes while you are reading a textbook assignment at home as it is while you're listening to a lecture in class. The same basic rules of selection apply in either case.

- Zero in on the key facts of each section and record them concisely in your own words in your notebook.

- Keep the notes as brief as you can-- there is no point in reproducing a handwritten duplicate of the textbook.

- Summarize in *your* words rather than the author's--this will help you to understand and remember what you have read.

- No matter how quickly you're jotting down notes, be sure your handwriting is clear enough to be readable when you have to refer to that information later.

- Keep your study notes for each course separate and clearly labeled so you can quickly find the ones you need when you're reviewing for an exam.

MAKE THE GRADE

Improving Your Memory

Note-taking
Note-taking is part of the process of learning and remembering. It helps fix the information in your mind as you organize and outline on paper the material you want to remember.

Repetition
The next step in the process is repetition. If you want to remember certain facts, reread your notes on those facts several times. Then put your notebook aside and write them down on a separate piece of paper or on index cards. You may want to use different colors for different subjects. Compare your results with the original notes to find out how much you remembered and what you have to spend more time on.

Using All Senses
Memory experts recommend using as many of your senses as possible when you are learning new information. Some suggest, for example, that you read aloud rather than silently when you are trying to memorize something because then you hear the words as you see them, and one sense reinforces the other.

Timing

Some experiments indicate that the best time to memorize is before you sleep rather than after. People tend to remember less of what they have studied early in the day than what they have concentrated on before bedtime. It's thought that sleep helps to set the information more firmly in your mind, while the distractions of a normal day tend to interfere with remembering what you learned in the early part of the day.

Keep in mind, though, that those experiments relate more to strict memorization than to general comprehension, so you certainly shouldn't rule out mornings as study times. But if there are a lot of dates or place names that you want to recall for a test, working on them before bedtime would be a good strategy.

Learning to Concentrate

One of the most useful skills you can develop is your ability to concentrate--to pay attention and absorb the significant elements of a given situation, whether it's a lecture, class discussion, or textbook assignment. With your powers of concentration working at peak efficiency you can devote more of your study and homework time to exploring subjects in greater depth or getting a term paper written without having to give up several evenings of television to do so.

Paying attention in class will not only help raise your grades. It will also give you more free time for pursuing a new interest, a part-time job, or a favorite activity.

One of the biggest stumbling blocks to concentration is anxiety, but there are a few simple things you can do to overcome that barrier. You can avoid a lot of anxiety by being well-organized and coming to class prepared. If you do the required work as it's assigned, study and review your notes regularly, you don't have to worry about being called on in class because you can respond with confidence. More important, you can devote your full attention to the material being covered in class that day.

Being an Assertive Learner

The best way to maintain concentration is to be an assertive, active learner. Here's how:

- Don't simply listen--take notes and ask questions.

- Speak up and ask for clarification if something isn't clear.

- Jot down comments and questions to yourself if the lecture prompts some train of thought you want to pursue independently--but do it quickly and stay focused on the subject under discussion.

It's definitely to your advantage to overcome whatever shyness you have about speaking up in class and asking questions. You can't be well prepared in a subject you don't understand.

Taking Class Notes

Another essential skill for successful learning is the ability to take clear, well-organized notes. The points covered in a class lecture are those the teacher considers most significant. Often they serve as a summary or outline of the course material. By listening carefully and making note of the key names, dates, and events discussed in each class, you are giving yourself a triple advantage--specifically, the opportunity to:

- Absorb information as you hear it
- Reinforce information as you write it and see it in front of you
- Review information at your convenience

It's a good idea to review your class notes each night rather than waiting until just before a test to go over three or four weeks worth of notes. Rereading notes the same day you take them:

- Helps to plant the information firmly in your mind

- Gives you a chance to identify immediately anything you haven't understood

- Eliminates the pressure of having to absorb massive amounts of information in a single study session

Learning from Past Performance

Virtually all students study *for* tests. Wise students also study *from* tests. When you get back a test paper, don't simply look at the grade and file it away. Go over every question. Reviewing those you answered correctly will reinforce that knowledge. Analyzing the questions you missed will give you a checklist of what you have to spend more time on and study in greater depth.

Try to think of tests in a positive way. Tests, after all, indicate what you know and have accomplished. They are also constructive guides to what you haven't quite mastered yet and have to devote more effort to. Use them as tools to work with and learn from.

OVERCOME TEST JITTERS

The best remedy for test jitters, of course, is being extra well prepared. There just is no substitute for knowing everything you need to know--and then a little bit more. But often even that is not enough to calm those jitters.

What Not to Do

Your first inclination is probably to quickly try to review all your notes, or borrow a classmate's notes to see if he or she has information that you don't have. Don't give in to that urge because it's bound to do more harm than good.

If there are certain facts you don't know five minutes before test time, you aren't going to learn them at that point in any way that will help you on the test. On the contrary, you are more likely to confuse yourself with odd facts that you can't relate to what you do know.

Give Yourself the Benefit of the Doubt

If you have done an adequate job of preparation, trust your understanding of the subject and your ability to deal with questions about it.

If you are not well prepared for the test, don't increase your liability by panicking. There's a good chance that just by having been in class and having taken notes, even if you have not reviewed them or completed all the required reading, you will know enough to get a passing grade. You may have to settle for the lowest possible passing grade, but that isn't as bad as failing, and you can compensate for it by being extremely well prepared for all future tests.

Remember as you sit down to take a test that it's only one small part of your overall grade for the course. That one test will not determine whether you pass or fail; it is not a matter of life and death, so keep the situation in perspective and try not to let test jitters cloud your mind.

Basic Test-Taking Techniques

■ Once the test is on your desk, read through it from beginning to end before answering any of the questions. Doing this will give you the advantage of knowing the length and range of the test so you can gauge how much time you can afford to spend on each part. Otherwise you might spend three quarters of the test period on the first two pages of multiple choice questions and not leave enough time for the two essay questions on the third page. Learning to pace yourself is an important test-taking technique.

■ The next step is to go through the test again, this time answering all the questions to which you know the answers. It makes sense to do this--both from a practical and psychological standpoint. Suppose the time is up before you have answered all the questions you are unsure of. At least you will get credit for the correct answers, some of which may be at the very end of the test. If you had stopped midway to struggle with the tough ones, you might never have gotten to the easier ones. The other advantage you give yourself is a sense of accomplishment. Once you've answered the questions you know, you have successfully completed a portion of the test and can work on the tougher parts with less anxiety.

■ On multiple choice or true/false questions, if you don't know the answer use your powers of reasoning and deduction to try to determine the correct choice. In a multiple choice question, one or two answers are often obviously wrong so you can eliminate them immediately and concentrate on deciding which of the remaining answers seems most logical.

You may find clues to the correct answer in some of the other test questions, which is another good reason for reading through the test before starting.

■ On a true/false series of questions it is harder to apply reason and logic to deduce the answer. You really have to know the information. But as a short-term expedient, if you are completely stymied on a particular question, it is better to guess (and have a 50 percent chance of being right) than to leave the question unanswered. Just don't rely on guessing, because you are bound to be wrong 50 percent of the time and besides, the whole point of being in class is to learn, not to guess the right answers to what you haven't learned.

■ On an essay question, if you don't know the exact information you are being asked to discuss, include what information you do know that may in some way relate to the topic. For example, if you are asked to write about Franklin D. Roosevelt's first term in office and can't remember his inauguration date, or the details of important legislation during that period, but you do remember facts you read about Roosevelt's family life or how hard it was for people to find jobs then because of the

Depression, write about those things. Doing that may help you to remember the more pertinent facts you have momentarily forgotten. At the very least, you may earn partial credit for what you do know even if it isn't precisely what you have been asked.

■ Whatever you do, write legibly. There is no point in giving correct answers that the person grading the test can't read. If your instructor has to struggle to decipher your handwriting, he or she may not be inclined to give you the benefit of the doubt when your answer is half right.

What to Do About Low Test Grades

Some very smart people just can't seem to overcome their test jitters so their test grades don't reflect what they actually know. If you have that problem--if your mind goes blank when you are handed a test paper, no matter how well prepared you are, you may not be able to completely master the skill of taking tests, but there are measures you can take to compensate for that fact.

You will have to work harder in other areas to make your instructors aware of what you know.

Here are some steps you can take:

- Speak up in class--be the first to volunteer answers to questions raised during class sessions
- Hand in every homework assignment on time and well organized
- Do the same for all reports and research papers due during the semester

If you think your test marks are going to lower your grade significantly, talk it over with the instructor. Explain the problem you have with taking tests--let your teacher know that you are concerned about the problem. You may be able to do an independent project or an extra assignment to at least partially compensate for low test grades. The instructor may also have some helpful suggestions for dealing with your test jitters.

USE SUPPORT SERVICES

Almost every student comes up against a problem subject now and then. What do you do when paying close attention in class and reading every textbook assignment diligently doesn't seem to work? That's the time to make use of your school's support services. Start with a visit to your academic adviser to get information about what's available and suggestions for how to proceed.

Learning Labs

Many schools have learning labs that enable you to work intensively and independently, using innovative approaches and sophisticated technology to help you improve in specific subject areas. If you're having problems with a foreign language course, interactive audio and video tapes are ideal ways to bring your skills up to par. They give you a chance to repeat material as many times as you need to master it and learn at your own speed. Videos can be very helpful, too, for getting a grasp on science course material that you may not have been able to keep pace with in class.

Learning labs are becoming increasingly computerized. In many schools you'll find a wide range of interactive software programs that you can use to improve your skills in anything from reading comprehension or creative writing to calculus, physics, or European history.

Take advantage of what your school has to offer--and do it as soon as you have any inkling that you're having trouble. It's much quicker and easier to overcome a small problem than one that's grown large while you tried to ignore it.

Peer Tutors

Some people find that one-to-one learning situations are more effective than studying independently. If you're one of those people, peer tutoring may be the answer for you. More and more schools encourage students to learn from one another by having students who are highly skilled in a particular subject work closely with students who are having problems in that subject.

Getting coaching and advice from a fellow student who's been through the same classroom experiences you have can give you a whole new perspective on mastering the subject. For some students it's the camaraderie of working with a peer that's appealing and helps them overcome stumbling blocks. For others, it's a sense of competition that prods them to catch up to--and perhaps overtake--the peer tutor as quickly as possible. The benefits of peer tutoring are often mutual, by the way. Many students who've acted as tutors report that it's increased their understanding of the subject and that they often discover new insights from the people they're helping.

The Library

Keep in mind that your school and public libraries are invaluable resources. They are not only a source of books and videos for entertainment and research; they're a mine of material to help you improve your academic skills. You'll find information in book and audio-visual form on how to:

- read, write, and speak more effectively

- conquer math anxiety

- improve your memory

- study more efficiently

Making good use of the libraries you have access to is an important part of going beyond school survival to school success.

Academic and Career Counseling

Lots of students turn to their school advisers only when they've hit a snag. Don't limit your opportunities in that way. The counseling staff at most schools have much more to offer than solutions to temporary problems. They're skilled professionals who can help you:

- chart an academic program that expands your options for the future

- explore special programs and activities that broaden your experience

- identify realistic academic and career goals based on your talents and interests

Be a self-starter when it comes to using the support services available to you. And if your school doesn't have a particular service that you think you and other students need, give your recommendations to the appropriate administrator. You may not get what you want because there isn't enough money in the budget or not enough students who share your concern, but you owe it to yourself to try.

YOUR COMPATIBILITY QUOTIENT

How do you rate in terms of compatibility? Do you get along well with friends, casual acquaintances, instructors, school administrators, classmates you think of as rivals? There are always going to be some people you like less than others--and some you really don't like at all. The point is that while you don't have to *like* all your classmates, fellow club or team members, and instructors, you do have to spend a lot of time with them, and you can accomplish your goals more efficiently and comfortably if you are on good terms with them.

Compatibility versus Popularity

There certainly is a relationship between compatibility and popularity, but you don't have to be everybody's Number One favorite person to get along with others. Just about everyone wants to be liked, admired, and complimented, but it is not realistic to expect those responses from everyone at all times. Often your classmates and instructors are preoccupied with their own concerns and too busy to notice all your sterling qualities. Some of the people around you are just not going to be temperamentally in tune with your personality--and there is no point in turning yourself inside out to win someone else's approval. If you suspect that you do this from time to time to boost your popularity, test yourself with the following quiz.

Compatibility Quiz

Your Behavior	Often	Some-times	Hardly Ever
Do you tailor opinions to agree with the person you are with?	____	____	____
Do you compliment others without really meaning it?	____	____	____
Do you pretend to like or dislike someone (or something) to impress another person?	____	____	____
Will you gossip about a friend to win some-one else's friendship?	____	____	____
Do you downgrade an-other's achievements to make your own look more impressive?	____	____	____
Do you do things you really don't enjoy just to be one of the gang?	____	____	____

Give yourself three points for every question checked in the **Often** column, two points for a check under **Sometimes**, and one point for each check under **Hardly Ever**. If your score is nine or more, the chances are that you are over-emphasizing popularity as a goal.

To get perspective on yourself and a sense of self-esteem, take a look at your own strengths. Make a list of them, being as objective as you can and not letting false modesty get in the way. Keep those qualities in mind when you start to think that everyone else is smarter, or better looking, or more successful than you are. Everyone (that includes *you*) excels in some area and has problems in other areas. Focus on being yourself--the best of yourself, of course--as you develop and expand your academic, creative, and social strengths.

The Fine Art of Listening

When you fantasize about the ideal you, what are the qualities you imagine you need to be popular and successful? Do you put academic brilliance, athletic achievement, good looks, and a flair for witty conversation right up at the top of the list? You might not even think of including the ability to listen on that list, but the fact is that being a good listener is one of the most important social and academic skills you can develop.

The academic advantages of listening are obvious. The more carefully you listen in any classroom situation, the more you will get out of the course and the more popular you will be with the instructor. Imagine what it's like to be a teacher lecturing to a room full of people, some fidgeting and being distracting, others staring vacantly into space--physically present but otherwise a million miles away--and still others obviously engrossed in what's being said and absorbing the information. It's not hard to guess which students will be most popular with that instructor.

The good listeners are going to be best prepared to ask intelligent questions and answer class-room and test questions correctly, which are two major ways a teacher gauges his or her own effectiveness as well as students' performance. And teachers, like anyone else, want reassurance now and then that they are doing a good job.

The social benefits of listening are equally rewarding. You are not alone in feeling awkward and tongue-tied when meeting new people, whether it's a group of classmates at the beginning of a semester, the staff of the student organization you've just joined, or unfamiliar people at a friend's party. From where you stand, it looks as if everyone knows everyone else. They all seem so much more confident than you feel. You've already forgotten the names of most of the people you were introduced to and you can't think of anything bright or funny to say.

The next time you are in that situation, try to remember that just about everyone is feeling some of the same kind of uncertainty you are. Some of them are probably looking at you a little enviously and wishing they could be as cool and together as you seem to be. With that in mind, go up to one of the people you've just met and if you can't remember the person's name, don't be afraid to say so, but be sure to listen carefully when the name is repeated and *remember* it this time.

Conversation is a two-way activity--you don't have to take responsibility for doing all the talking. And one of the best ways of launching a conversation is not with a barrage of witty anecdotes but with a thoughtful question that indicates your interest in the other person. Most important, once you have asked a question, *listen* to the response. There is nothing less appealing than someone who tunes out while you are talking, or who seems to be waiting impatiently for you to finish in order to continue his or her monologue. If you are really listening, you are bound to find that you and the other person share some interests, and once you have made that discovery you won't find it hard to make conversation.

Getting Along With the Powers That Be

How you get along with classmates and fellow team and club members are key factors in your school career, but equally important are relationships with school authorities. Because they seem to have such power over your life, you may forget now and then that instructors and school administrators are human beings too. They have their good and bad days, their pet peeves and personal enthusiasms. In general they are intelligent, reasonable adults who want to do their jobs as well as possible. They have spent a lot of time as students themselves in order to gain the knowledge needed to teach and advise you. They are likely to be helpful and supportive if you give them a chance--by being cooperative, attentive, and reasonably well-prepared.

You may find an occasional instructor whose demands on you seem unreasonable. Don't waste your time or energy in a battle of wits with that person. It's a battle you are almost sure to lose since the advantages of authority and experience are on the instructor's side. Instead, make up your mind to be extraordinarily well-prepared for that instructor's class; don't give him or her the slightest excuse to be critical of you. Think of it as a challenge to your own ingenuity and you may even find it fun. With a lot of consistent hard work you might make an ally of that instructor. At the very least you will avoid criticism, establish a solid background in that particular subject, and get some good practice in dealing with difficult people.

GET YOURSELF IN FOCUS

Self-awareness is one of the most important factors in surviving and thriving in school and beyond. Getting to know yourself is an on-going process, so the time to start practicing your self-analytical skills is right now.

On the Surface

Classmates, friends, and family may be able to give you some objective opinions about how they see you, but it's hard for others to be completely frank about your good and bad points. Besides, they see only a part of you--the exterior you choose to show and perhaps some of the inner thoughts you are willing to share with them. Feedback from people you trust helps you to understand yourself, but it also takes some self-study to know where your strengths and weaknesses lie, and what to do about them.

Look Inside

Start by making two lists--one identifying all the good qualities about yourself and a second including all the things you don't like about yourself. When you make the lists, don't let false modesty hide the things you like about yourself. After all, this information is for your eyes only, and it's important to have the clearest picture possible. The same goes for negative points. You can't do anything about altering them until you've identified them. Your lists might read something like the following:

Good	Not So Good
honesty	procrastination
sense of humor	bickering with friends
lots of energy	shyness
imagination	stubbornness
loyalty	poor in foreign language
good at most sports	sloppy writing skills

Accentuate the Positive...

First, look at your strong points and decide how you can make each work for you in getting the most out of school. Then analyze the weak points to see how you can overcome them. Here are some random examples of what you might come up with based on the sample lists above.

Honesty
All or most of the people you know probably share the basic traits of honesty. They don't steal or lie. But being honest covers a wider range of behavior than that, such as not copying on an exam or letting a classmate copy from you; making your homework and special assignments entirely your own work and not cribbing from someone else; not making excuses for poor test results, lateness, etc.; or speaking

up when you don't understand something in class even if it embarrasses you. Honesty encourages trust--and being trusted is bound to boost your self-confidence.

Sense of Humor

This is one of the strongest assets you can have. Being able to laugh instead of gripe about your day-to-day experiences keeps you and the people around you in good spirits. You can't always avoid disappointments but a sense of humor will keep you from being shattered by them and get you back on track more quickly.

Imagination

If your sense of humor is accompanied by a lively imagination, so much the better. Think of ways you can take a fresh, imaginative approach to your school work. If you're having trouble with a subject, try teaching it to someone else. Your best friend might be a willing pupil. Take it step-by-step from the beginning. You'll be surprised at how much you do know, and organizing the information to teach to some-one else helps you to understand it better.

Energy

Energy is what fuels your day-to-day activities. Concentrate on harnessing your energy and imagination to a disciplined schedule and school will be a snap. Dogged plodding or frantic spurts of activity are poor substitutes for a balanced program of work and fun.

Good at Most Sports

If you're skilled at sports, you've found a wonderful way to keep physically fit, make friends, and be a campus celebrity. Athletic skills may come easier to you than academic studies, but don't slight one for the other. If you don't make the grade in class, you'll find yourself barred from the team until you raise your average, so don't let it slip in the first place.

Procrastination

If you procrastinate you are one of the vast majority of people who postpone the inevitable. Make a pact with yourself *now* to stop putting off assignments you know have to be done eventually. Begin today with one task. Don't wait until next week to read the book you have to report on in two weeks--start reading it now. That will give you more time to prepare your report, which will probably result in a better paper and a higher grade.

Poor in Foreign Languages

Few people do equally well in *all* subjects, but by following a few basic rules you can get acceptable grades in any course.

- Don't waste time and energy hating the subject.
- Do homework for the problem subject first while you're most alert.
- Try to find some aspect of the subject that appeals to you or that relates to a subject you like and do well in.

Sloppy Writing Skills

You may never become another Shakespeare but you can learn to write clear, grammatically correct sentences and organize them in logical sequence to express the theme of an essay assignment or the information you want to include on a test. Start by deciding what you want to say and outline it point by point. Then state each point in the most direct way possible, using specific words, not vague terms.

Be your own editor. Keep a dictionary and grammar book nearby and use them whenever you're unsure. The skills you develop will help you in all your courses. Your lecture notes, term papers, and essay questions on exams will all improve once you focus on *what* you want to say, in what *order*, and *how* to say it in the most direct way.

Knowing your strengths and weaknesses is the first step toward putting your strong points to work for you and getting rid of those self-made stumbling blocks.

Self-Evaluation Chart

Good

Not So Good

_____ _____
_____ _____
_____ _____
_____ _____
_____ _____

Your Headstart on the Future

Your student years are a time to learn, expand, and refine the knowledge you'll rely on in your future career. They are also a time to develop:

- practical skills
- responsible attitudes
- good habits

Being well-organized fits all those categories. The better organized you are, the more you'll get out of your course work, extracurricular activities, social life, and work experiences. So concentrate on getting organized to achieve more now and throughout your future.